HEAVY HAULAGE
AND ABNORMAL LOADS
VOLUME 4

First published in 2000 by
Roundoak Publishing
The Old Dairy,
Perry Farm,
East Nynehead,
Wellington,
Somerset
England TA21 ODA

Tel. +44 (0)1823 461997
Fax +44 (0)1823 461998
www: nynehead-books.co.uk
email: info@nynehead-books.co.uk

Design by
Roundoak Associates

Printed in England by
Acanthus Press,
Wellington, Somerset

Front cover: Looking resplendent in the mid morning sunshine during October 1999 was this new DAF 95XF 480hp 6x4 Spacecab tractor operated by MSM Heavy Transport of Keighley, West Yorkshire. The vehicle is pictured at rest on Taunton Deane Services (M5) undertaking one of its first jobs, which involved the movement of this 60 tonne Caterpillar 350L long reach demolition excavator from Manchester to Plymouth. Rated for 150 tonne operation V778 LUM was coupled to a Nicolas 2 bed 4 modular trailer for the 108 tonne GTW haul.

Rear cover: The demolition of Plymouth's Blue Circle cement factory at Plymstock saw the extraction of a 122 tonne cement mill drum. At 14ft diameter the load presented quite a handful for its transporter H.C. Wilson of Elmswell, Suffolk. They utilised a new Scheuerle/Nooteboom Flatcombi 9 axle modular trailer to move the load a short distance to nearby Victoria Wharf for onward shipment to Spain. The move took place during August 2000 and was undertaken by a 160 tonne capacity Scania 143E 8x4 tractor unit.

Half title page: Pictured on the M5 Taunton Deane Services in Somerset during March 2000 is this Volvo FH16 6x4 Globetrotter 520hp double drive 150 tonne tractor belonging to Chris Bennett of Wilmslow, Cheshire. R384 BJA was on this occasion hauling a NCK Nova HC65 crawler crane weighing 62 tonnes, from Liverpool to Devonport dockyard. The trailer was a 4 axle rear steer Nooteboom fitted with a single axle jeep dolly.

Title page opposite: Number 188 in the Sunters of Northallerton fleet was this 75 ton capacity Scania LBT 110 day cabbed tractor unit. Powered by a DS11 250hp engine, the vehicle is pictured during October 1975 moving the body of an American 999 crawler crane from London to Middlesbrough aboard a 50 ton capacity Crane Fruehauf tandem axle low loader.

Below: Pictured leaving the works of Blight & White structural engineers in Plymouth with a large 95ft long 16ft wide lattice roof girder are Somerset based Gillards Transport of Burrowbridge. Loaded upon a tri axle 'home built' rear steer bogie, the frame was one of two such pieces hauled to Croydon railway station during March 1991. Traction came courtesy of an immaculate 80 tonne capacity Volvo F12 6x2 unit.

HEAVY HAULAGE
AND ABNORMAL LOADS
VOLUME 4

DAVID LEE

ROUNDOAK PUBLISHING

INTRODUCTION

Moving a load from A to B may be a straightforward job but when the load becomes abnormal it can present all sorts of problems. The term 'heavy haulage' can often be a bit misleading in reality, as some loads are not necessarily heavy, but do present problems with oversize dimensions either by length, width or height. An abnormal load then, to give it its correct description, consists of any oversize item which would put any vehicle transporting it outside Britain's Construction and Use regulations and into the current Special Types General Order (S.T.G.O.)

Having to contend with masses of bureaucracy and red tape, the heavy haulier tends to portray himself as an elite operator, indeed getting an abnormal load on to the road can prove to be more of a problem than the actual move itself. Police notification must be given two clear working days in advance if the load to be moved is in excess of 80 tonnes gross, 2.9m.wide or longer than 18.65m. Each police force area through which the load will transit needs to be informed, along with the relevant highway and bridge authorities, Railtrack, and in the case of high loads the area's electricity and telephone companies.

Over the years the size and weight of plant and machinery has increased significantly, but the most common section of abnormal load work continues to be the Category 2 range, covering movements between the scale of 30-50 tonnes gross. Tractor units employed on this type of work vary from 6x2 layout, well capable of loads grossing up to 60 tonnes, or the more heavy duty double drive 6x4 units, handling loads above this weight. The heavier Category 3 sector certainly qualifies for the use of the latter, but due to critical plating issues regarding axle weights, operators are now specifying more 8x4 tractors to undertake these duties. Vehicles operating on public roads grossing above 150 tonnes, or moving loads measuring over 5.0m.wide must also obtain special approval from the Ministry of Transport who will issue a VR1 form prior to the move taking place, giving the necessary authorisation. This is also the case for a load measuring over 27.4m. in length when being transported by a single vehicle/trailer. Usually loads of these dimensions are made known to the haulier well in advance of their planned movement, and in some instances dimensions are submitted prior to the load even being built in such cases as generators, pressure vessels, bridge beams, boats etc.

In many aspects the abnormal load haulier is very similar to the heavy crane operator, each utilising expensive and highly specialised machinery. Indeed, the two bands of personnel can often be seen working 'hand in hand' forming an elite team of 'shifters and lifters' offering complete packages for the movement and installation of heavy equipment. German manufacturers seem to dominate the market of big telescopic crane production with Demag and Liebherr being the two leading builders. Such heavy cranes often run at transportation weights around the 100 tonne mark, and are therefore also classed by the authorities as an abnormal load. Many larger models run on multi axled chassis to significantly reduce axle loadings imposed on the road surface.

There will always be oversized loads that need moving and the financial rewards for executing such tasks are certainly there to be had. However, after costly investment in specialist equipment to undertake such work each operator must obtain the maximum use from it. Let's hope that the next decade will bring forth such optimism, and that the haulier will not become a further victim of revised legislation, costly delays and high fuel prices - all of which they have certainly had to sustain during the past ten years.

I have had the great pleasure of meeting many enthusiasts since my interest in heavy haulage began, thirty years ago. I would like to mention each one individually but the task would be endless! However, three names immediately spring to mind which have resulted in the formation of strong friendships. They are Adrian Cypher, Marcus Lester and Richard Tew. In their company I have spent many enjoyable hours with regard to our mutual interest in road haulage. Long may it continue.

Once again, I have selected the last three decades from 1970 to date, to form the basis of this book; although I make no apology for giving more coverage on this occasion to current heavy haulage vehicles which are constantly being renewed or upgraded. As well as numerous company personnel I would also like to thank the following individual people who have kindly afforded me so much help and co-operation by way of supplying previously unpublished photographs or information:- Bruce Blacktopp, Jean-Paul Cammaerts, Jim Campbell, Kevin Cobb, Phillip Dyke, Adrian Goodman, Paul Hancox, Steve Higgins, Bev Hitchcock, Arthur Ingram, Dave Kinsella, Jon Lauder, Cameron Mason, Cliff Marsh, Andrew Park, Stephen Pearson, Martin Phippard, Leo Pratt, Jim Richie, Len Rogers, Graham Stewart, Rodney Tew, Denis Tomlin and Johan van de Water. Particular appreciation is expressed to Roy Knight for the invaluable help given to me during the past seven years.

In closing I would like to take this opportunity of thanking my wife, Sandra, for enduring my constant heavy haulage escapades up and down the country. I am sure this volume will prove that my travels have been worthwhile!

David Lee
Plymouth, October 2000

April 1998 saw J. B. Rawcliffe of Mawdesley moving their heaviest load to date at the Cammell Laird shipyard, Birkenhead. The 245 tonne mid ship section in course of building was destined to become a mobile drilling rig, and moved out of a fabricating shop about half a mile along a public road and craned into a dry dock to marry up with previously built sections. With a height of 40ft and a width of nearly 50ft the load was moved upon 2 rows of 10 axle Nicolas platform trailers pulled by the company's four axle Scania 143E 450hp and ERF EC14 500hp 40 tonne ballasted tractors. The overall gross weight of the transport was 385 tonnes. *D.Tomlin*

5

Above: This well worked Atkinson 'Silver Knight' 4x2 32 ton tractor belonging to Heanor Haulage was powered by the ubiquitous Gardner 180 engine and used by the company on 'light' low loader work. Photographed in May 1974, the crew are securing a prototype Terex motor grader to its tandem axle King drop frame trailer, en route to Scotland.

Right: Parked at Redbridge lay-by heading out of Southampton during March 1975 was this Atkinson Viewline 6x4 55 ton capacity tractor running in the Pickfords fleet, based at the company's Sheffield depot. Sat upon a tandem axle King 35 ton capacity low loader was a fully rigged Smith C2835 34 ton crawler crane which had been used at a nearby sewage station project. Several Viewlines were operated by Pickfords during this period all featuring 250hp Cummins engines and six speed transmissions.

Above: Although Pickfords operated the largest number of Atkinson Viewline tractors, other two and three axle versions found their way into other British haulage fleets. This example was owned by Ogden Plant who operated primarily as demolition specialists. Again, Cummins powered, the 6x4 unit was coupled to a knock-out back axle Crane low loader carrying a 30RB crawler crane when pictured during March 1975.

Left: As well as running Atkinson 6x4 units featuring the Viewline cab, Pickfords also operated some of these 4x2 ballasted tractors. Pictured in April 1975 is AMH 539H entering its own depot at Millbrook, Southampton, using a Crane 'four in line' dolly to move a new GCI 5400-L mobile hydraulic self erecting tower crane. This load had just been collected at 201 berth having previously crossed the Atlantic from its manufacturers in Canada and was destined to be demonstrated at a major U.K. plant exhibition prior to entering service with a renowned crane hire company.

9

Above: This Atkinson 6x4 tractor has had an interesting life, having originally been operated by a Midlands tanker haulier as a 6x2 twin steer 'Leader' unit. When purchased from Stoke-on-Trent based Wild Transport in the early Eighties by P. H. Antell and Sons of Shillingstone, Dorset, it was converted to 6x4 'Venturer' spec. and given a 65 ton capacity rating. With a sleeper cab conversion undertaken by Wynns of Newport 'Dreadnought's' Gardner 240 hp engine was uprated to 265 hp and coupled to a 15 speed Fuller gearbox. Pictured at a Cornish steam engine rally during June 1985 KLG 287L sports a 'Searcher' radiator badge which is a bit misleading as this was Atkinson's 6x4 rigid model. Sat aboard the tri axle King low loader was a Fowler compound roller and a Garrett engine. The Atkinson was eventually sold in 1990 to showman Alan Ford in Sussex who used the vehicle to transport his 'Wall of Death' presentation.

Left: Bridon Ropes of Darlington operated this 75 ton Atkinson Venturer 6x4 tractor powered by a Cummins NTK 290 engine. It was one of two such tractors employed by the company during 1975 to move this 45 ton cable reel down to Devonport dockyard. Pictured at rest on the A38 near Ashburton, the outfit utilised a tri axle Task low loader to move the heavy duty cable which was destined to be fitted to what was then Europe's largest dockside crane, nearing completion at the yard's new submarine refit complex.

12

What must surely be one of the most popular trucks ever produced was the renowned Bedford TK, launched in September 1960 and remaining in production until 1984. This example was fitted with a custom built ballast box for drawbar boat transportation by Portsmouth based Ken Brown. The cruiser being moved on this occasion during June 1973 is passing over the Brockhampton Lane bridge above the A27 Havant by-pass. Loaded aboard a purpose built tri axle boat trailer, the vessel was en route to the Halmatic premises which at this time were situated at the nearside foot of this bridge. This Bedford tractor was originally new to Faulkners Plant Hire of Waterlooville.

Transports Specioux Valla, based near Lyon, France, operated this Berliet GR250 4x2 tractor fitted with the 'Relaxe' steel cab introduced in 1959. Still in the livery of its original owners Transports Creuzy, both operators specialised in the movement of large steel sheets and cylinders etc. until our Ministry of Transport frowned on the use of standard 4x2 tractors hauling tandem axle trailers often grossing over 50 tons. Having to comply with UK axle weight requirements, both companies suddenly became rare visitors but in August 1979 Valla collected this 30 ton Henley forklift truck body which was exported to France using a tri axle drop frame trailer built by Kaiser.

13

Econofreight were awarded the contract to move four long loads from Loughborough to Southampton docks during April 1981. The 38 ton 80ft long crane beams were moved using a variety of equipment including the pair of Dyson low line steerable bogies shown. Providing the traction for this particular load was a DAF 2805 DKS 6x4 ballasted tractor which featured Allison automatic transmission. Rated for 100 tons the DAF is pictured awaiting off-loading of the Morris crane beams at 206 berth. *D. Kinsella.*

Jack Hill of Botley operated a pair of these DAF 2800 cabbed 6x4 heavy haulage units during the late seventies/early eighties. The FTT 2805 DKS tractors were good for 100 ton operation but in this instance during May 1980 the vehicles were employed on much more mundane work transporting these overhead travelling crane beams which were two of four such loads moved from Loughborough to Southampton for export to Hong Kong. Pictured prior to unloading at 205 berth in the Solent container terminal RJT 512R was working in conjunction with a tandem axle '8 in line' Crane bogie whilst LVS 83P utilised a tri axle 'home built' bogie. *D. Kinsella*.

Above: Formerly operated by civil engineering contractor Edmund Nuttall, this DAF 3300 6x4 150 tonne capacity tractor was sold to nearby heavy haulier P. H. Antell and Sons from Shillingstone, Dorset during February 1990. This picture taken a decade later shows the tractor engaged in moving a pannier tank steam railway locomotive from Swindon to Bodmin during May 2000. It was loaded aboard a 60 tonne capacity Belgian built Faymonville 4 axle rear steer low loader.

Right: The load pictured was to form part of the giant Pepsi Max rollercoaster ride at Blackpool's Pleasure Beach seafront complex. The structure was one of several such pieces built by Watsons of Horwich, near Bolton, and assembled on a site near Blackpool Airport during October 1994. Each section was then moved along the promenade to the jobsite and craned into position. As Watsons are part of the Amec Group, it was Amec's transport division, along with Rawcliffe's, who undertook the movement of the loads. The DAF 3600 6x4 tractor shown used a 4 axle Nooteboom extendable trailer to move this 28ft high by 24ft wide section along the short route. Several items of 'street furniture' had to be temporarily removed and the relevant telephone and electricity companies were also present to lift their respective cables aloft whilst the load passed beneath. *D. Tomlin*

Using a DAF 3300 6x4 tractor unit, Gloucestershire heavy haulier John Golding was responsible for moving this pair of 120ft long roof support girders which was one of two such loads moved through Plymouth during June 1989. Supported at the front by a bolster attached to the tractor's fifth wheel with a 'home built' tandem axle rear steer bogie at the back, the loads were moved out of their fabricators at Cattedown to a new leisure complex under construction in the city centre.

Dutch heavy transporter Van Den Herik of Naarden is seen here just prior to boarding the Brittany Ferries ro/ro vessel 'Val De Loire' at Plymouth ferry terminal during August 1995. The 37 tonne railway coach was heading for Spain to undertake some track research work being hauled by a DAF 95 430 6x4 Spacecab tractor unit. The modular trailer upon which the load was transported is a 2 bed 4 Nooteboom fitted with an extended beam deck featuring integrated railway lines built into its bed.

Above: The DAF 95XF range was introduced into Britain during April 1997 and one of the first double drive heavy haulage tractors to enter service was this FTT 480hp unit belonging to Bolton based Amec Plant and Transport. Shown pulling its 4 axle Grafton low loader and jeep dolly the outfit was moving an IHI CCH 500-2 crawler crane from Scarborough to Brixham when pictured on the M5's Taunton Deane Services during March 2000.

Right: The first DAF95XF 8x4 tractor to enter UK service joined the Allelys Heavy Haulage fleet during May 2000. One of the first jobs it undertook was the movement of this 105 tonne Class 37 freight railway locomotive from Plymouth to Nottingham using 12 rows of Goldhofer modular platform trailer. Powered by a 480hp engine the Superspace cabbed tractor is rated for 250 tonne operation when running as a drawbar unit as shown here. The second steer axle was salvaged from the former Cadzow owned DAF 95 380 8x4 tractor J761 FYS which was previously destroyed by fire. The axle conversion and fabrication of the additional stowage lockers and fuel tanks together with the chequer plate wings were carried out by Leyland based T.Vac. The temporary ballast box featured an Atlas loading crane and when fitted gives the tractor a weight of around 42 tonnes.

Above: J. J.Bullen Heavy Haulage of Appley-Bridge, Lancashire, put this 150 tonne capacity DAF 95XF Superspace cabbed unit into service during May 1999. Powered by a Cummins 530hp engine, the vehicle is delivering a Liebherr 944 scrap handling machine into Preston Recycling during August of that year aboard a tri axle Nooteboom low loader. The 40 tonne load had been collected from Ashton-in-Makerfield, Manchester. *D. Tomlin*

Left: This Spacecabbed DAF 95XF 6x4 tractor entered service with Moveright International of Coleshill, Birmingham during August 2000. Rated for 200 tonne operation the aptly registered W200 TON 480hp unit's first job was moving this HST powercar out of Laira, Plymouth. The 70 tonne Class 43 locomotive 'County of Cleveland' was to be hauled to Crewe upon a 5 axle rear steer extendable low loader comprising a King neck and rear bridge joined together by the company's existing modified main integral rail deck. Moveright specialise in the transportation of railway related equipment including locomotives, carriages and other rolling stock.

Above: Demag's AC1600 18x8 500 tonne capacity crane weighs 108 tonnes when in travelling mode. Power comes via a 560hp OM 443 engine coupled to a ZF transmatic box.One of Hewden Stuart's Demag AC 1600's was sold to Dublin based Crane Hire Limited during September 1999. Registered M602 UNW, the crane is pictured just off the A1 near Peterborough en route to Liverpool for shipment across the Irish Sea.

Left: Pictured stopping over at the company's Blantyre yard en route from Grangemouth to London during April 2000 with a 45 tonne Zeppelin tracked piling rig is this Cadzow Heavy Haulage DAF 95XF 6x4 tractor. Rated for 150 tonne capacity the Spacecabbed 530hp unit was put on the road during October 1999. It's 4 axle Nooteboom low loader features a single axle jeep dolly and is capable of moving loads of up to 80 tonnes. *S. Pearson*

25

Left and above: The Demag AC2000 is unique due to the fact that for a machine of its size it can travel with its full main boom in position. Rated for 800 tonnes lifting capacity, the 18x8 108 tonne crane is driven by a 571hp Daimler Benz OM 502 LA engine linked to an Allison CLBT 755 electronic transmission and torque converter. All axles are fully steered apart from line 6, making the vehicle easily manoeuvrable. It features a fully powered five section 60 metre main telescopic boom with the option of utilising a 24-96 metre additional luffing jib. Hewden Crane Hire took delivery of their AC2000 in January 1999, and it is pictured heading for Cornwall's Eden Project site at Bodelva to undertake the lifting of four 5 tonne air handling units. The crane was rigged with 40 metres of main boom and a 90 metre luffer to place the equipment onto the roof of the dome shaped geodesic conservatories. *Above:* The Leyland based Ainscough machine pictured at Crick joined its company's fleet in January 2000.

Above: Originally operated by HM Plant of Bridgwater, N400 HMP, an ERF EC14 6x4 Olympic cabbed tractor passed on into Runtech Heavy Haulage ownership during March 1998. Based at Port Talbot, South Wales, the 80 tonne capacity unit is pictured during January 1999 moving a 30 tonne Aveling Barford RD40 dumptruck from Bristol to Helston, Cornwall, using a tri axle King low loader to do so.

Left: It was a rare sight to witness Leicester Heavy Haulage using their 135 ton capacity ERF MW cabbed 6x4 unit as a ballasted tractor on drawbar operation. However the truck was utilised in this manner during October 1980 to move this turbo alternator down from its builders Brush Electric at Loughborough to Southampton docks for onward export to South Africa. Coupled to 8 lines of Cometto modular axles, the Cummins powered 335 hp tractor still remains in company ownership although it has now been withdrawn from active service. *D. Kinsella*

Above: Photographed prior to unloading this 32 tonne Caterpillar 631B motor scraper at Felixstowe docks for onward export during March 1999 was this ERF EC14 6x4 unit belonging to Brennan and Coates. Based at the company's Langley Moor, Co. Durham depot, the high cabbed Olympic unit is capable of 80 tonne operation. Coupled to an Eaton 16 speed gearbox is a 14 litre Cummins 475hp engine, well capable of moving this load down from Thetford using a King tri axle low loader. *A. Goodman*

Left: Rated for 80 tonne operation is this ERF EC14 6x4 Olympic cabbed tractor owned by RBL Haulage of Warrington, on contract to Powerscreen. Fitted with a Bonfiglioli PS 1400 14 tonne/metre truck mounted crane and running on super single tyres all round, the vehicle is a regular visitor to the annual Torbay Waste Management Show held at Paignton. For the 1998 show in June the ERF provided the traction to exhibit this 20 tonne Powerscreen 615LL Trommel tandem axle recycling plant.

31

Left and above: Cadzow Heavy Haulage of Blantyre, Scotland, operate a pair of ERF EC14 8x4 Olympic cabbed tractors on abnormal load work. The first unit joined the fleet during May 1998 and was subsequently followed by the second in January 1999. Both are powered by N525E Cummins Celect engines and feature ZF Ecosplit 16 speed gearboxes and Sisu built axles. Plated for 200 tonne operation the ERF's also boast steering/lifting second axles and heavy duty front and rear towing jaws. The first picture *(left)* shows R552 GNS at rest on Charnock Richard Services (M6) during July 1999 carrying a 69 tonne Terex TR100 dumptruck from Motherwell to Southampton for onward export to Indonesia. The trailer was a 5 axle Goldhofer STZ-VH extendable low loader. The second picture *(above)* again taken on Charnock Richard Services, depicts S747 BGD, the latter EC14 8x4 to enter the Cadzow fleet. This is pulling a 4 axle Nicolas low loader laden with a 75 tonne Hitachi EX800H excavator heading for Harthill, Lothian, in April 1999, having been collected in Bridgwater, Somerset. *D. Tomlin*

33

34

Entering service during October 1997 this 80 tonne ERF EC14 double drive tractor is used to haul a 45 tonne Wirtgen 2100DC road planer by its owners Tetlaw Contracting of Newton Abbot, Devon. Fitted with a 525 hp Cummins engine, the tractor has been matched with a Belgian built Faymonville four axle semi low rear steer trailer giving the loaded outfit a gross weight of 67 tonnes. A unique cradle mounted on the back of the tractor's cab accommodates the elevator of the planer when in transit. This technically enables the unit to 'steer' the overhanging shute when the machine's boom is left in the 'free flow' unlocked position, thus avoiding dangerous forward projections when cornering.

Leicester Heavy Haulage are the operators of this ERF EC14 6x4 Olympic cabbed 200 tonne capacity unit that entered service during January 1999, joining an impressive fleet of ERFs which already featured a similar example of the type. Power comes via a 525hp Cummins engine driving through an Eaton gearbox which enabled the unit to deliver this electric generator into Exeter's Marsh Barton power plant construction site during April 1999. As an articulated tractor the unit is permitted to move loads of 165 tonnes GTW although on this occasion all up weight was only 130 tonnes. An 8 axle 130 tonne capacity Nooteboom rear steer trailer was utilised to haul this load down from its manufacturers at Loughborough.

36

Rather a rare breed on UK heavy haulage was the Fiat 300PT 6x4 tractor, an example of which is shown here, originally bought new by V. C. Cooke & Son of Beccles, Suffolk during March 1976. The 300hp unit was good for 100 tons although when this picture was taken in June 1979 the Cat 621B motor scraper weighed only a modest 30 tons. The load was delivered into Plymouth's Millbay docks for export to Spain and moved upon a tri axle Crane Fruehauf low loader. When the outfit was eventually sold in May 1980 the tractor returned to its native Italy whilst the trailer found a new home in Ireland.

The arrival of Italian heavy hauliers through Southampton docks during the late seventies witnessed the continuing trend of operators using rigid 6x4 vehicles to pull short modular semi trailers via drawbars. Not only did the British authorities question this type of combination for its ability to move heavy loads, they were also interested in the manner that parts of the load were carried upon the flatbeds of the towing vehicle - acting as ballast! This Peyrani outfit is a typical example of such practice, pulling a sheeted load of 14ft wide factory machinery upon a 6 axle Cometto platform modular trailer. Providing traction was a Fiat 697N 6x4 44 ton GTW rigid powered by a 260hp engine.

Above: With a ballast body built by Boughtons of Amersham which included a 400 gallon auxiliary fuel tank, this Foden S40 cabbed 6x4 tractor was owned by Hallett Silbermann of Hatfield. With a capacity of 100 tons the 270hp Cummins powered unit regularly achieved one mile to the gallon when loaded, according to its operator. The drawbar low loader consisted of a King deck with removable swan-necks at each end supported by a pair of Scheuerle tandem axle 'eight in line' steerable bogies. With an 80 ton payload the trailer was well below its limit whilst hauling this Manitowoc 4000W crawler crane body from Manchester to Milford Haven during 1973.

Right: Pictured undertaking a local haul near Consett during 1977 were these two Foden S40 tractors belonging to R. Oliver (Plant Hire). Loaded aboard the 'hybrid' drawbar trailer supported at either end by a pair of tandem axle bolsters was a Bucyrus-Erie dragline crane minus its boom and tracks. Both Cummins powered Fodens were fitted with temporary ballast bodies for the move -TPT 377K as lead tractor occasionally assisting ADC 24K which was the main drawing unit.

38

Above: Making light work of climbing Hoads Hill on the A32 at Wickham, near Fareham, Hants during February 1975 was Jack Hill's Botley based Foden S40 6x4 120 ton capacity tractor, UFU 937J. Riding aboard a tandem axle King 60 ton low loader was the body of an NCK 1485-S crawler crane. Hills were to operate two of these double drive Fodens, the other being distinguished by its sleeper cab.

Right: Although civilian registered, this Foden S40 6x4 tractor operated under the auspices of the Military Vehicle Engineering Establishment based at Chertsey. Powered by a Cummins NTK270B and featuring Foden's own 12 speed gearbox the outfit was used to transport both complete vehicles and a wide range of components to military evaluation sites. Seen at Weyhill, near Andover during 1978, the load, in this instance riding upon a military specced Crane Fruehauf tri axle trailer, was the aluminium chassis of a tracked personnel carrier.

42 Based at Pickering, North Yorkshire are Slaters Transport, once a subsidiary of the Tilcon group, running a predominantly Foden fleet. During the early Seventies Managing Director Arthur Slater and crew entered his yacht 'Prospect of Whitby' into the annual Southern Cross Cup Blue Water race, which consisted of a series of four legs, the last of which was a 650 mile run from Sydney to Hobart, Tasmania. Arthur's yacht, together with Ted Heath's 'Morning Cloud' are pictured here, en route from the Hamble estuary near Southampton, to Liverpool, for onward shipment. Transport was provided by Slaters 240hp Gardner powered Foden S70 cabbed twin steer 6x2 38 ton tractor and one of the company's S36 cabbed Foden 4x2 units.

CKL Transport of Halifax operated this Foden S81 sleeper cabbed 6x4 tractor up until 1990. Formerly operated by civil engineering contractor Wimpey, the truck was rated for 100 ton operation and powered by a 335 hp Cummins engine. Riding aboard its King tri axle low loader when photographed during November 1989 was an NCK Pennine crawler crane being delivered into a new pumping station construction site at Marine Drive, Scarborough. *L. Pratt*

Above: Travelling through Somerset on the A38 high load route near Uffculme, avoiding the M5 motorway during April 1998 was Aberdeen based haulier Bob Milton. The load was one of two 16ft diameter water storage tanks moved from Peterhead to Plymouth aboard tri axle Broshuis step frame trailers. Pictured is a Foden 4400 6x4 unit but also involved was the company's Volvo F12 6x2 tractor sporting a unique Foden high roof conversion as shown on this vehicle.

Right: Based in Shanklin on the Isle of Wight is this Caterpillar powered Foden 4400 6x4 unit which works in the George Jenkins fleet. Shown during September 1998 at Smithaleigh lay-by on the A38 near Plymouth it had transported this 45 tonne Komatsu PC450LC excavator across from the island at Sandown via the ro/ro ferry link at Portsmouth. Formerly owned by Bristol haulier Graham Fear, the truck was coupled to a tri axle Andover low loader fitted with a King swan-neck.

Peterborough based C.D. Fisher are regularly employed moving concrete bridge beams out of a local concrete works at Tallington. Prior to running a Volvo F12 this Foden 4410 6x2 twin steer tractor was employed on this work. Fabricated from a former 20ft skeletal trailer was a single axle 'bonus loader' which, when coupled to the unit's fifth wheel, converted the vehicle to 8x2 spec. The 50 tonne 90ft long 'u' beam shown was awaiting unloading at a bridge construction site at East Sleekburn near Blythe. Supporting the back end of the load was a tri axle 'home built' rear steer bogie - formerly a Seddon Atkinson 401 6x2 tractor converted by R.W.S. at Plymouth.

The unusual load sat aboard this 5 axle Goldhofer trailer originates from Finland, and is a Tana 40F landfill refuse compactor weighing 40 tonnes. It was shipped over to the UK unaccompanied via Dartford where it was then collected by Osmond's Transport from Brenchley, Kent. The company used an 80 tonne capacity Foden 4410 6x4 Cummins powered tractor to then haul the machine to South Devon for the annual International Waste Management Show. The picture shows the load's arrival at Paignton which has had its blade and cab temporarily removed for easier passage to the exhibition site.

47

Above: R.J.C. Transport are based in Bedford and have been regular DAF operators for some time. However, the company now runs several Fodens on abnormal load work including this 4500 6x4 unit photographed at the Hillhead Quarry plant exhibition in Buxton during June 1999. It was pulling a tri axle Nooteboom semi low loader carrying a Komatsu-Moxy MT40B 28 tonne 6x6 articulated dumptruck. *R. Tew*

Right: Ainscough Crane Hire of Leyland operate several of these Foden 4525 XL high cabbed 6x4 tractors primarily used to haul crane counterweights and accessories with Nooteboom ballast trailers. This 5 axle example features rear steering and an extending deck which accommodates the 60 tonne telescopic boom from the company's Liebherr LTM 11000DS 1000 tonne capacity mobile crane. The tractor features Sisu tandem drive axles and Hendrickson rubber suspension. It is powered by a 14 litre Cummins 525 hp engine coupled to an 18 speed Fuller gearbox. *D. Tomlin*

Above: The Ford Cargo 6x2 38 tonne tractor unit first appeared in 1981 as a replacement for the 'D' series. Examples of this marque engaged on abnormal load work however, have always been scarce. One such vehicle did enter service with Somerset based Martin Hayman who employed it on agricultural machinery delivery prior to selling it to 'Mad Bert' a nearby scrap recycling specialist based in Greenham. The sleeper cabbed 3824 249hp unit is pictured here in the livery of its second owner coupled to a 27 tonne tandem axle Parker RWO 850DH mobile crusher in March 1999 - one of two operated by the company.

Left: This 30 ft. diameter 60 tonne subsea cable reel was transported internally at Peterhead harbour (North base) during October 1999 from its storage area to be 'loaded out' onto a ship destined for the North Sea oil production fields. Traction was provided by a Foden 4455 6x4 XL cabbed 150 tonne capacity unit belonging to Taylor Heavy Haulage, one of two such vehicles operated by the locally based company. Taylor also operates a fleet of mobile cranes under the Peterhead Crane Hire guise. The tri axle low loader used for the move featured here was a King. *S. Pearson*

51

Weighing in at 476 tonnes this 192 ft long SIF vacuum column was at the time claimed to be the largest load ever to be moved on a British public road. The short two mile haul took place during July 1981 along the B3053 and was destined for the nearby Esso oil refinery at Fawley having been previously shipped over from Holland. Suspended between two sets of Scheuerle 8 row modular bogies, the load was initially pulled by TRL 924H, Mammoet Econofreight's Mk I Scammell Contractor. Having joined forces with Econofreight the previous year Mammoet also supplied a tractor in the shape of a Dutch built FTF F8.28D 448 hp Detroit V12 powered 6x4 ballasted unit. Sporting Mammoet-Stoof livery the 100 tonne capacity tractor double-heading with the Contractor was one of six such models built and featured an Allison CLBT 5960 transmission and TC 690 torque converter.

Ginaf are a Dutch specialist truck builder based in Ederveen. Pictured is the company's 8x8 F480 tractor unit belonging to Lastra Heavy Transport of Breda, Holland. Fitted with a DAF engine and cab and a ZF gearbox, the ballasted tractor is depicted here at work in Britain when Lastra moved this 620 tonne petrochemical column. At 430ft long, it was at the time the longest load ever to be moved on a British road. The column was built by SIF-Holland in Roermond and shipped via canal to Rotterdam and onwards across the North Sea to Grangemouth for installation at the nearby BP Chemical Plant. The picture shows part of the short haul with the Ginaf pulling two sets of 14 row Nicolas modular axles each accommodating the load at either end. In reverse at the rear was a Lastra operated Mercedes 3850 tractor.

53

Weighing in at 100 tonnes in travelling mode is the Gottwald AMK 500-93 18x8 crane with its main boom being transported upon a smaller AMK 400 14x8 carrier. March 1991 saw this example owned by Castleford based Hewden Stuart on site at Marsh Mills, Plymouth prior to positioning several steel bridge beams to form a new flyover for the A38. Powered by a Mercedes Benz 520 hp engine the crane was capable of a 500 tonne lift using its three sectioned telescopic boom.

Benco Transport are based in the Devon fishing town of Brixham and have been operating since 1990 specialising in factory removals and boat transport. July 2000 saw the company about to move this motor boat from nearby Kingswear on the River Dart to the Thames and Kennet marina near Reading. It was carried upon a King tri axle air suspended step frame trailer which has been modified by Benco for boat transport having had its central section of bed removed to accommodate keels. The Iveco Eurotech 400E 38 6x2 380hp tractor features a 'Medium' roof sleeper cab and a Hiab 30 tonne/metre crane which greatly assists in loading/unloading operations.

55

Above and right: A pair of cancelled orders saw two Iveco 380 E47 8x4 Eurostar high roof 'Alto' cabbed tractors become available during the end of 1998. Originally converted from long wheelbase Eurotrakker 6x4 rigid chassis, they were rebuilt into 8 wheel tractors by North East Truck and Van who also fitted the additional second steer/lifting axles. Plated for 150 tonne operation, the units are powered by a 470 hp engine driving through a ZF 16 speed Ecosplit gearbox. The first example *(above)* joined the Elmswell based fleet of H. C. Wilson in Suffolk during March 1999 and is seen here in June 2000 at Washington Services on the A1(M) near Sunderland. The load is a 41 tonne Terex TR60 dumptruck en route from Motherwell to Teesport for export. The 55 tonne capacity dumper was riding upon a 5 axle Nooteboom beam deck rear steer trailer featuring a tandem axle jeep dolly. The other Eurostar *(right)* was put into service by Hill and Son of Botley, Southampton, during April 1999. It is pictured during June 2000 leaving Warminster, Wiltshire; home to the Royal Tank Regiment's 'A' Squadron. The 63 tonne Vickers Challenger 2 battle tank named 'Achilles' was loaded aboard a Nooteboom 5 axle semi low loader which was used to haul it to London to appear in a commemorative ceremony in Whitehall.

Above and right: The Iveco Eurotech 440E 42 6x4 tractor is rated for 100 tonne GTW operation and the type is a relatively rare sight on U.K. heavy haulage operations. However, two examples of the 420hp unit are shown here. The first, *(above)* pictured during August 2000 at Woodall Services on the M1 is operated by Chris Wright (Baildon) Ltd of Bradford. Coupled to a tri axle Broshuis step frame trailer, it was en route from Peterborough to Dewsbury, West Yorkshire with a boiler. The second Eurotech *(right)* was in service with V. C. Cooke & Son Ltd of Beccles, Suffolk when photographed at the SED Plant Show near Milton Keynes during June 2000. Its load was a tri axle 40 tonne waste shredder destined for delivery to an infill land site at Lackford near Bury St. Edmunds. *R. Tew*

Sunseeker International of Poole, Dorset are the builders of luxury boats which can be seen in harbours and marinas all over the world. The first mode of transport to their new owners, however, is often overland on the back of one of Sunseeker's low loaders. Hauling the new vessels all over Europe is this Iveco Eurostar LD 400E 47 6x4 'Alto' cabbed tractor which entered service during August 1999. Rated for 80 tonne operation, the 470hp unit was matched with a new Nooteboom tri axle rear steer extendable trailer.

Vanguard Vehicle Services (now TSL) of Leeds undertook the site movement of this 130 tonne Manitowoc Vicon 4600 dragline base machine during October 1990 at Taylor Woodrows Butterwell open cast mining site near Newcastle. A modular 2 bed 5 Nicolas trailer was used for the relatively short haul pulled by F785 TCP, a Leyland DAF 95 380 6x4 tractor unit. Also providing assistance as rear pusher tractor was a Volvo F12 ballasted to 30 tonnes. Gross weight tipped the scales at 212 tonnes. *D.Tomlin*

61

Although this underground storage tank only weighed 8 tonnes, its oversize dimensions made it an awkward load to get to its delivery address in South East Cornwall. The Midlands regional depot of Beck and Pollitzer based at Bilston were responsible for the move from Shrewsbury to Torpoint during March 2000. Coupled to a tri axle Broshuis extendable step frame trailer, was a 66 tonne capacity Leyland DAF 95 430 6x2 Superspace cabbed tractor both pictured here at Saltash Services on the A38 just west of the Tamar Bridge.

Photographed during May 1999 at the abnormal load lay-by on junction 16 of the M6 motorway were Lincoln based KDJ Heavy Haulage moving a 75 tonne Hawker Siddeley transformer. The load had been collected in Walthamstow and was destined for a new power station then under construction at Winnington, Cheshire. The 119 tonne GTW haul was undertaken by a 150 tonne capacity Leyland DAF 95 430 6x4 Spacecab tractor unit coupled to a Broshuis 2 bed 4 trailer fitted with air suspension. *R. Tew*

Above: Pictured at Exeter Services on the M5 heading for the Plym Valley Railway in Plymouth during March 2000 were Studley based Allelys Heavy Haulage. The 105 tonne Class 37 diesel railway locomotive had been loaded out of Bescot, West Midlands, onto 12 rows of Goldhofer modular axles. With a total gross weight of 182 tonnes the traction came courtesy of a Leyland DAF 95 380 6x4 unit previously operated by Ainscough Crane Hire but now upgraded for 200 tonne GTW operation.

Right: Pictured in the company's revised red, grey and white livery prior to leaving the Hillhead Quarry plant show at Buxton during June 1999 is this well presented Leyland DAF 95 430 6x4 Spacecab unit owned by Wilmslow heavy haulier Chris Bennett. Coupled to a tri axle King low loader, the vehicle was to move this 26 tonne Fiat Hitachi EX 255 excavator to its new owners in Manchester. *R. Tew*

Above: Liebherr's LTM 1400 16x8 telescopic mobile crane has a lifting capacity of 400 tonnes. Power comes via a Daimler Benz OM44A engine producing 530hp, to move the 96 tonne vehicle. The Hewden Stuart Castleford based crane was photographed at rest on Leicester Forest Services (M1) during June 1999. The crane features a one boom pivot section and three telescopic sections, giving a lifting height of 50 metres. With the addition of a luffing lattice jib the overall lifting height can be increased to 84 metres.

Right: With a lifting capacity of 500 tonnes this Baldwins operated Liebherr LTM 1500 mobile crane was heading for Devonport Dockyard when pictured on the A38 at Smithaleigh near Plymouth during April 2000. Grossing 96 tonnes the 16x8 telescopic crane features steering on axles 1 to 4 and 7 and 8. The carrier is powered by a 8 cylinder Liebherr 598 hp engine which drives through on Allison CLBT 755 automatic transmission giving 5 forward speeds and 1 reverse.

THE MILLENNIUM LIFTER
AINSCOUGH
AINSCOUGH
AINSCOUGH
HEAVY CRANE DIVISION
01772 622116
THE MILLENNIUM LIFTER
AINSCOUGH
AINSCOUGH
R73 NHG
LIEBHERR

Left and above: Based on Liebherr's successful LTM 1800 16x8 crane chassis is the LTM 11000DS/LGD 1550 1000 tonne capacity models in service with Ainscough Crane Hire and Baldwins Industrial. Working with a telescopic boom the crane is designated an LTM 11000DS, whilst rigged with a conventional lattice jib it becomes an LGD 1550. Powered by a Liebherr 570hp engine linked to an Allison CLBT 755 automatic transmission the crane weighs 96 tonnes when in transit. The Ainscough crane *(left)* christened 'The Millennium Lifter' is seen during July 1998 en route to Plymouth to lift a fishing boat into the River Tamar. The Baldwins machine *(above)* is pictured at South Mimms Services (M25) having undertaken some overnight lifting in central London during July 1998.

Left and above: The Lorain Moto-Crane range originates from Ohio, U.S.A. Part of the Koehring International Marketing Company, the cranes were sold in the U.K. by Vales Plant at Watford who were the appointed British agents. The 100 ton and 90 ton capacity models which were the MC9115 and MC 790 respectively proved popular with all the major crane hire fleets, with Bowmer and Kirkland, Grayston, Sparrows and the British Crane Hire Corporation all taking deliveries of these machines. At 11ft wide these mobile cranes were amongst the largest of their type being moved on the road at that time, weighing in at around 50 tons. The BCHC MC 9115 *(left)* was to assist in the initial stages of demolition of Portsmouth power station in May 1973, whilst the Sparrows MC 790 *(above)* was about to be rigged at Plymouth's Millbay Docks during June 1980 to lower a 50 ton pontoon into the water.

71

Above: XSU 410S was one of several Mack tractors operated by Coatbridge based West of Scotland Excavations. Much of the company's work originated from the nearby Terex U.K. assembly plant in Motherwell which is where this pair of 72-51 wheeled loading shovels had been collected. The FM 786 ST 6x4 tractor was good for 150 ton operation and used a tri axle WNC built low loader to haul the machines down to Southampton for shipment to the Middle East. *D. Kinsella*

Right: Pictured climbing up the A62 across the Pennines near Delph is Chris Millers renowned 240 ton capacity Mack Interstater Aerodyne cabbed tractor 'Bonzo Bear'. Fitted with a Maxidyne 300 hp engine driving through a 12 speed gearbox and torque converter NFV 803T was hauling a Cometto girder frame trailer running on two sets of five row modular axles. The 14 ft wide load was one of six 150 ton water flow valves moved from their manufacturers Markhams of Chesterfield to the CEGB Dinorwic pumping station located inside the Elidir Mountain in Snowdonia. Providing back up as push tractor was Millers 150 ton Volvo F88 6x4 unit PHY 21M ballasted with concrete blocks.

Above: ACK 645V was the second Mack tractor owned by Worcester based Powells Tractors. The FM786 Aerodyne cabbed unit replaced RBN 147S, a standard cabbed Interstater 6x4 unit in 1984. Pictured at Leigh Delamere Services on the M4 hauling a NCK Atlas crawler crane from Dudley to Reading during July 1985 aboard a Bridge tri axle low loader, the unit was rated as a 150 tonner. Originally operated by J. B. Rawcliffe the tractor when sold by Powells entered the nearby Allelys Heavy Haulage fleet at Studley. From there it was sold and subsequently converted into a heavy recovery truck based in the Manchester area.

Right: Dutch heavy haulier Van Den Herik of Naarden were previously known as F.I.R.S.T. from Amsterdam. The company withdrew from heavy haulage in 1997, but their Mack MH613 Ultraliner 6x4 tractor is pictured here on a visit to Britain during June 1995 on the M40 near Oxford. Loaded aboard a 9 axle Nooteboom modular trailer was a crated section of factory machinery heading for a delivery in Birmingham. *C. Marsh*

Above: Work to widen and strengthen the Tamar Suspension Bridge which connects Cornwall and Devon at Plymouth began in July 1999. Heading for this project the following October is this steel truss which was one of four similar pieces built by Cleveland Bridge in Darlington. Econofreight Heavy Transport of Middlesbrough were given the task of moving these loads which were positioned in specially constructed tilted cradles welded to the trailer bed. The MAN 33 422 6x4 150 tonne tractor shown here in Econofreight's revised logo was coupled to a 6 axle Nicolas semi low loader to accommodate the 50ft long load.

Left: Pictured beneath the jib of the big floating crane barge 'Mersey Mammoth' in Liverpool during August 1998 was another impressive Dutch operated Mack MH 613 Ultraliner 6x4 ballasted tractor belonging to Team Heavylift of Dordrecht. Loaded upon its 11 axle Scheuerle platform trailer is a 150 tonne boiler destined for the Bridgewater Paper Company in Ellesmere Port. The 50ft high by 37ft long load was one of two identical boilers delivered by sea from their manufacturer in Utrecht, Holland. The Team Heavylift Group was founded in the mid 80's consisting of various companies based in Holland, Britain, Norway, U.S.A., Oman, Pakistan, Singapore, and Saudi Arabia.

Above: August 1997 saw Malcolm Plant's MAN 32 422 6x4 150 tonne tractor taking a break on the M74 Hamilton Services during the movement of this 50 tonne Liebherr 962 excavator from Houston, Renfrewshire to Motherwell, Lanarkshire. Based in Brookfield, the tractor was coupled to a 60 tonne capacity Transquip 4 axle low loader which features a sloping sawn-neck specifically designed to ease the transport of motor scrapers. *C. Mason*

Right: Joining the Newark based heavy haulage fleet of Markham Moor Transport in August 1996 was this 150 tonne MAN 33 463 6x4 tractor. Powered by a 12.8 litre engine driving an Eaton 16 speed gearbox the F2000 series Roadhaus cabbed unit is also fitted with a Telma retarder. P631 SFW is seen here in September 1999 prior to crossing the River Avon at Bristol heading for Chard, Somerset. Grossing 125 tonnes, its load consisted of a dairy processing vessel which had been transported from Dunfermline upon a 8 axle Broshuis extendable semi low loader. *S. Higgins*

Above: This Canadian Erin Fingerscreener 165T track mounted mobile screening machine was collected from Torbay's waste management exhibition at Paignton during June 2000 by its new owner John Mould of Reading. The 25 tonne machine had just been loaded alongside the seafront onto the company's tri axle low loader built by Andover. For the traction a MAN 33 403 6x4 unit was utilised.

Left: August 1998 saw the arrival of a MAN 33 463 double drive tractor into the Blantyre based Cadzow Heavy Haulage fleet. The 460bhp Roadhaus cabbed unit is rated for 100 tonne operation but is shown here only grossing around 70 tonnes moving a Liebherr 952 excavator out of Hamilton during April 1998. The tri axle low loader trailer was a Task.

Above: Parked in Allaway Avenue, Portsmouth during April 1974 was M. Sewell's Bawtry based Mercedes LPS 2024 6x2 38 ton tractor unit. Fitted with a 240hp 6 cylinder engine and 6 speed gearbox, the unit was taking the weight of a 60ft long 25 ton concrete beam destined for a bridge construction for the M27. The tandem axle '4 in line' rear steer bogie is of particular interest, being very robust and seemingly of German design, possibly utilising Scheuerle running gear.

Left: Formerly operated by owner driver Paul Weedon working for Rotherham based THB, this MAN 32 422 6x4 Roadhaus cabbed tractor passed into the Collett Heavy Transport fleet during August 1998. During September the following year the 150 tonne capacity unit was fully ballasted to 40 tonnes to move this 140ft long overhead crane beam out of Morris Cranes at Loughborough to Sizewell power station in Cumbria. The 38 tonne beam was supported on three and four axle Scheuerle modular bogies each fitted with turntable bolsters.

84

Collett Heavy Transport of Halifax purchased this Mercedes 3544 8x4 200 tonne tractor unit from a dealer in Holland. Originally operated by Dutch boat transporters Van De Wetering, the 480hp unit is shown coupled to the company's Scheuerle Inter Combi hydraulic modular trailer assembled in 2 bed 4 configuration. The load being moved during June 1999 was one of two 74 tonne electric generators, transported from Rugby to Barrow. The trailer's vessel carrying deck was used for this job, its two outside beams ideally giving support to the generator.

Peterborough Heavy Haulage of Yaxley, operated three of these Mercedes 2650 6x4 150 tonne capacity units on low loader work. Named 'Nene Riguenbach' this vehicle was the third of its type to enter service with the company, who are now part of the C.E.L. Group. Riding upon the Nooteboom 4 axle low loader and tandem axle jeep dolly is a 70 tonne Hitachi EX700 excavator which was being moved from Langley to Devonport dockyard during October 1999. Due to bridge weight restrictions in force at the time on the M5 near Bristol, the load was routed along the A34/A303 into Devon and is seen at Cartgate Services near Yeovil prior to commencing the final leg of its journey.

Above: Now part of the Initial Plant Services group Grayston White and Sparrow Crane Hire are now operating several of these Mercedes 2644 6x4 tractors. Plated for 120 tonne operation they are normally to be found pulling 5 axle Broshuis ballast trailers carrying the accompanying cranes counterweights and accessories, as shown here. Power comes via a 435hp 14.6 litre V8 400 series engine linked to a Telma retarder which is ideally suited to a combination regularly grossing around the 100 tonne weight scale.

Right: Grossing some 233 tonnes, this German owned outfit belonged to Bohnet of Munich who moved a large casting out of Riverdon Castings at Sheffield to Immingham docks during November 1997. Using a Mercedes 3553 8x4 Eurocabbed tractor unit and Goldhofer 13 axle modular trailer, the outfit was assisted on the latter leg of its journey by a DAF 95 430 6x4 ballasted unit acting as push tractor and owned by Lincoln based KDJ Haulage. The load is pictured on the A15 outside RAF Scampton, near Lincoln. *R. Tew*

Above: With their head office in Castleford, West Yorkshire, Hewden Stuart Crane Hire used this Mercedes 2644 6x4 tractor to transport the telescopic boom of their 800 tonne capacity Leibherr LTM 1800 mobile crane. The 60 tonne jib is positioned upon a specially constructed cradle mounted on a 5 axle King stepframe extendable rear steer trailer.

Right: V665 NUM is one of six Mercedes Actros 3353 6x4 tractors operated by Castleford based Hewden Crane Hire which entered service during late 1999/early 2000. Rated for 120 tonnes, the units are matched with Nooteboom 5 axle semi low extendable trailers with rear steering. This particular vehicle is seen during July 2000 on the A30 just west of Okehampton, Devon, carrying ballast weights and associated tackle for the accompanying Demag AC2000 800 tonne capacity mobile crane. Three of the trucks are based at Castleford including the one pictured. The remainder operate from Hewden's Dartford, Heathrow and Manchester depots.

Above: TSL-Vanguard Heavy Haulage of Leeds operate five Mercedes Actros 2540 6x2 72 tonne capacity tractors. This example is resting on the M61 Bolton North Services in March 1998 whilst hauling a 24 tonne tunnel shaft support fabrication from Scunthorpe to Eire. The specialist vessel carrier Goldhofer tri axle trailer features hydraulically operated extending side beams with a non floor bed and a carrying capacity of 54 tonnes. *D. Tomlin*

Right: Certainly an unusual sight at the time in Britain was this Austrian operated Mercedes Actros 3553 8x4 tractor unit operated by Wels based Horst Felbermayr. Originally leaving the Daimler Chrysler production plant in Worth, Germany as a 6x4 2653LS unit, it was subsequently converted to 8x4 specification by Doppelmayer in Austria with the fitment of a mid-lift second axle. The load pictured, grossing 46 tonnes, was a steel bunker for delivery into the Port Talbot waste treatment works in South Wales during March 2000. The 5 axle step frame trailer was a Nooteboom. *R. Tew*

Pictured prior to leaving the Site Equipment Demonstration show at Milton Keynes during June 2000 was this Mercedes Actros 3343 6x4 80 tonne capacity tractor belonging to Cotton Transport of Swadlincote, Derbyshire. The Bell Equipment liveried vehicle was put into service during May of that year specifically to move this manufacturer's products which are built nearby at Burton-on-Trent. In this instance the load sat aboard the tri axle King trailer is an 18 tonne Bell B30C 6x6 27 tonne capacity articulated dumptruck. *R. Tew*

Photographed having just disembarked from a North Sea ro/ro ferry into the U.K. during May 1999 was this impressive German owned Mercedes Actros 3353 (Titan conversion). Operated by Baumann Schwertransporte of Bornheim-Hersel, the load was one of several trams destined for delivery to Croydon that had been built in Germany and carried over upon a 4 deck 4 Goldhofer modular trailer. Acting as ballast for the tractor unit was a set of heavy duty steel ramps which were to be utilised in the off loading operation when the load arrived at its destination. *R. Tew*

Developed by Nicolas of France, the hydraulic self propelled electronically controlled (Hy-Spec) transported system consists of 4 and 6 axle line units which can be operated individually or in multiple combinations to suit the load to be moved. With a 36 tonne axle load per line the system has the ability to rotate 360 degrees giving maximum manoeuvrability. In this instance 18 lines of Hy-Spec axles were utilised to move a 1700 tonne ship section measuring 100ft wide by 140ft in height. The transport took place at Barrow shipyard during September 1999 and involved the short public road movement from a yard fabrication shed to a nearby slipway for final assembly. The complete outfit was being remotely controlled by the operator on foot pictured to the rear of the load. *C. Mason*

The Oskosh Truck Corporation of Wisconsin, U.S.A. started in 1917 initially manufacturing all wheel drive trucks for off road work. The company quickly became established for building specialised vehicles for oilfield, firefighting, snow plough, timber and heavy haulage work. This R04E 1234 6x4 80 ton capacity tractor was built in 1968 by the company's South African subsidiary, Barlow Oskosh. Operated by McCormack Macnaughton of Belfast, who at the time were main Caterpillar agents, BIJ 5727 featured a Cat 325hp engine, Spicer 16 speed gearbox and a 100 ton capacity winch. Photographed coupled to its tri axle 60 ton capacity King folding neck low loader carrying a pair of Caterpillar 941B tracked loading shovels, the truck was eventually sold to a dealer in South Wales in 1980 where it was converted for heavy recovery work. *P. Hancox*

Founded in 1907 as Austro-Fiat, OAF produced Italian designed vehicles prior to developing its own trucks after the Second World War. Changing its title from AF to OAF, the specialist Austrian builder based in Vienna now has close ties with MAN in Germany, resulting in licence built MAN designs featuring on many of their products. This MAN cabbed OAF 48 792 tractor is one of the most powerful units ever to be operated in Europe, powered by a V12 800hp engine. The 8x8 tractor was involved in the transport of this 80 tonne EBG transformer from Linz, Austria to Truro, Cornwall during May 1999. Riding upon a Goldhofer 7 axle modular trailer, the load is seen awaiting the arrival of a police escort near Bodmin on the A30.

Bonneted American conventional trucks, whatever make they may be, are always guaranteed to turn heads on British roads. One such vehicle high on presentation must surely be this 1980 Peterbilt 359 6x4 unit operated by Dave Atkinson of Raisbeck, Cumbria. Powered by a Cat V8 550hp engine the prime mover is seen during May 1997 at Plymouth docks having just loaded these military vehicles - a Leyland 4x4 5 tonne truck and a Steyr-Daimler-Puch Pinzgauer Turbo D 4x4 Truck Utility Medium (HD) - and was bound for the Royal Marine camp at Arbroath. Its tri axle Nooteboom step frame trailer features an extended neck to accommodate the 48 tonne capacity tractor.

Above: Pictured having just arrived at Southampton's ferry terminal on a sailing from Le Havre was this Renault TRH 350 6x4 tractor belonging to Vassel S.A. of Tassin, France. The V8 350hp powered 150 ton tractor was pulling a tri axle Kaiser heavy duty low loader laden with a 40 ton 'Sea Horse' which is used for subsea cable laying within the off-shore oil industry. *D. Kinsella*

Right: Hamnett Haulage are based in Halifax, West Yorkshire and operate this Renault Major R420 6x4 130 tonne capacity tractor. Coupled to a Belgian built 4 axle Faymonville low loader, the unit was used to transport this 60 tonne Mk I Challenger battle tank from Worcop MOD training camp in County Durham to Catterick Garrison camp in North Yorkshire. *A. Goodman*

Above: The Peterhead Crane Company acquired the ex-Cadzow Renault Major R385 6x4 Turboliner tractor during 1998. Good for 90 tonne operation the vehicle is pictured at Barton Services on the A1 coupled to a Broshuis 5 axle ballast trailer transporting crane counterweights and associated tackle from one of the company's Leibherr mobile cranes.

Right: Plated for 80 tonne operation is this Renault Magnum AE 385 double drive tractor in service with Tilbury based Pinch Plant. Coupled to a Nooteboom tri axle step frame semi trailer its load when seen during March 1998 was a 25 tonne Soilmec R208 tracked piling rig destined for delivery in London.

At the time this Rosenkranz 600 ton capacity truck mounted crane was the largest of its type available for hire in the U.K. Built in Germany during 1971 it could be rigged with a 160 metre tower rig assembly or a standard 97 metre main boom. Imported into Britain by Baldwins during 1975 its 16x10 chassis is based on a Faun KF400 83/99 prime mover powered by a 530hp engine and Allison 12 speed semi automatic gearbox. Grossing 90 tonnes in travelling mode the crane is pictured at Southampton's 'old' docks during December 1977 prior to undertaking the dismantling of an elderly large dockside crane. Over the years the crane was continually uprated, first to 800 tons and then to 1000 ton capacity. It was eventually withdrawn from service due to a major failure.

Built in Brighton locomotive works in 1878 this 0-6-0 Terrier Class engine 'Newport' spent its emergent years operating as a shunter. Following its conversion to an A1X with the fitment of a larger boiler and coal bunker it was moved to the Isle of Wight rail network until 1947 when it returned to the mainland. Having been condemned in 1963 it was bought by Butlins Pwllheli holiday camp as a static exhibit. During 1973 however the 32 ton loco returned to the Havenstreet Isle of Wight steam railway and is pictured in Portsmouth prior to boarding the ferry. Traction came via Pointers ex Hamblins Scammell Highwayman pulling a Dyson knock out back axle low loader which was still based at the old Hamblin Anstey Gorse depot at the time. Once on the island the loco was refurbished and today works regularly carrying many visitors on the Havenstreet to Wootton line.

Above: Seeking to determine the ideal type of power unit for their specialist operation, Heanor Haulage fitted Cummins and Detroit diesel engines to their Scammell Contractor 6x4 units during the early Seventies. PNU 772K, a lightweight Contractor, was later to become HHT 001 an 8x4 tractor fitted with a Volvo F88 cab. It is seen here in its former original guise - prior to its sleeper cab conversion - being powered by a Detroit 8V71N engine and 15 speed Fuller transmission. The tandem axle trailer, based on an original American Rogers design for military operations, was modified by Heanor with the fitment of an extra wide deck for the safe movement of plant such as motor scrapers. Two motive power units from such machines, namely Caterpillar 631Bs are seen here prior to export to Malaysia.

Left: Transporting a 200 ton transformer on their Crane Fruehauf 12 axle 300 ton capacity girder frame trailer during November 1974, Pickfords are seen here just emerging from the Shedfield to Droxford road just north of Wickham, Hampshire on the A33 which was part of the defined heavy load route pre M27. The lead Scammell Contractor PGO 711E was one of the first batch of 240 tonners to be operated by Pickfords in 1967. The pusher tractor, sporting the company's revised lighter blue livery, was a 100 ton Contractor. The load was being moved from Rownhams sub station near Southampton to Portsmouth dockyard for onward ro/ro shipment.

105

Photographed traversing Chailey cross roads near Haywards Heath, East Sussex, en route to the Bluebell Railway in October 1971 was Sunters first ever Scammell Contractor pulling a Nicolas 4 deck 4 modular trailer. Transporting an 86 ton 'West Country/Battle of Britain' Bulleid Pacific steam locomotive, TPY 675H was fitted with a 14 litre Cummins pushing out 335hp through an RV30 semi automatic gearbox. After nearly eight years of rugged service the vehicle was taken off the road during 1978 for a complete rebuild. An entire engine/transmission overhaul followed prior to the truck being sent to Plaxtons in Scarborough for a total cab rebuild. When it re-entered service with its narrower ballast body it was given the revised registration mark YVN 308T. The Scammell was eventually exported to India during the late Eighties to work for the Lift and Shift operation there.

Pickfords Heavy Haulage in action at Scott Lithgow's Cartsburn East shipbuilding yard at Greenock in October 1981. The load, an M.O.D. test vessel had been hauled into the fabricating shop in the normal manner, but having undergone extensive modification the vessel's weight had increased to 550 tons (600 tons including the weight of supporting cables and slings). This made it impossible to return the boat to the River Clyde via the slipway previously used, so Pickfords Nicolas modular equipment was used to overcome the problem. This was arranged as a 12 line double width module giving a 24ft wide platform. The boat loaded safely onto the trailer, a pair of 240 ton Scammell Contractors BCN 318V and XUU 919T, being a Mk1 and Mk2 respectively, hauled the load to the jetty. From there the vessel was lowered into the water by Sparrows 1000 ton capacity Gottwald crane.

Above: Starting life in Roche, Cornwall with MCC Plant this 240 ton Scammell Contractor was originally fitted with a fifth wheel and ran as an articulated unit. In 1973 it was acquired by Jack Hill of Botley to haul his Crane 200 ton capacity girder trailer. After the fitment of a ballast box and crew accommodation by way of a Cat D8 cabin, it was put to work hauling various items such as this NCK Atlas crawler crane. Pictured in Woolston in April 1975 'Betsy', as she was affectionately known, was sold in 1976 to Billingham based Magnaload, who later became Mammoet Econofreight.

Right: The arrival of the Scammell Contractor in 1964 was to eventually take Wynns of Newport to new horizons. It proved an ideal replacement for the company's ageing Pacifics and Diamond T tractors, the basic Leyland LAD cab design, although primitive by today's standards, being highly respected by drivers and crew alike. This 240 ton Contractor is pictured during October 1974 moving an 82 ton transformer across the A29 at Billingshurst Sussex, following a very circuitous route from a sub station at Chessington, Surrey. The load's final destination was Chichester and it was moved with the aid of a 110 ton capacity Crane 6 axle girder trailer. Bringing up the rear was a second standard cabbed Mk I Contractor.

Above: Reputed to be one of the last day cabbed Mk I Scammell Contractors to leave the Tolpits Lane production line is this unit HBB 775W, based internally at N.E.I. Parsons, Heaton, Newcastle. Pictured during November 1994 hauling a 70 tonne stator shell on 8 lines of Nicolas axles, this Contractor was one of two operated inside this location, the other being a former Wynns tractor, GDW 848E.

Right: Making its debut at the 1976 Commercial Vehicle Show in Earls Court was this Wynns Mk 2 Scammell Contractor 'Superior' shown here parked on the service road at Southampton docks during May 1977. The 350 ton capacity Nicolas girder frame trailer was laden with a 280 ton transformer bound for the CEGB power station at Fawley. Having been off loaded from the ro/ro vessel 'Aberthaw Fisher' the previous day, the load was about to begin its short journey via a complex route assisted by 'Dreadnought' a Mk 1 Contractor as push tractor. Once on site the transformer was off loaded and another identical redundant one brought back to the docks to be shipped to Goole aboard the same awaiting vessel.

Above: February 1996 saw one of the largest loads ever to be moved out of the Air Products factory at Acrefair, Wrexham. It was a 204 tonne 17ft diameter LP column destined for export to Rozenburg, Holland. With a gross weight of 310 tonnes Econofreight used their 40 tonne Scammell Contractor Mk2 'Challenger' to move the 182ft long load to Ellesmere Port with the aid of two sets of Nicolas modular axles. They were assembled as 9 and 8 row modules at the front and rear respectively. A second Scammell tractor - Scammell S26 'Evening Star' was used to 'double head' along sections of the route which included a steep climb up the A539 towards Whitchurch.

Left: This ex Wynns Scammell Contractor GTX 211N was bought by Abnormal Load Engineering of Stafford. Rated for 240 tons it is pictured reversing a 117 tonne Cowans railway crane up into the hold of an Atlantic ro/ro ship at Southampton docks during September 1990. Destined for export to South Africa 'Resolute' had hauled the load down from its builders N.E.I. Cranes at Carlisle aboard 10 rows of Nicolas modular axles. A total of 1,257 Contractors were built by Scammell, the last of which entered service during 1983. *D. Kinsella*

113

Above: UYL 809S was one of five Scammell Crusader 6x4 sleeper cabbed tractors operated by Pickfords Heavy Haulage. Based at the company's Ipswich depot fleet No M9508 is shown here prior to unloading a 40 tonne capacity Terex 33-07 dumptruck that was destined for export to the Middle East during 1980. Coupled to a tandem axle King 35 ton capacity low loader the V8 Detroit powered tractor was good for 65 ton GTW. *D. Kinsella*

Right: The Scammell Crusader CR100 6x4 unit commonly known as the 'Amazon' was rated for 100 tons. Powered by a Rolls Royce Eagle engine and Fuller 15 speed gearbox AHB 807T was one of six such vehicles belonging to Wynns of Newport. The outfit is pictured gently inching under a pedestrian footbridge at Totton whilst moving a 53 ton storage vessel, which was one of two such loads being moved at the time during July 1985. Loaded aboard a 6 axle Nicolas extendable trailer the tank was en route to the nearby Fawley oil refinery complex.

Above: Based at Pickford Industrial's Birtley depot GNB 941Y was one of two Scammell S26 40-35 6x4 tractors operated by the company - the other being GNB 940Y based in Glasgow. Fitted with a Cummins NTE 350 engine driving a 12 speed Spicer box and torque converter the unit was built for 150 tonne operation. It is depicted here pulling a 120 tonne capacity Nicolas 2 bed 4 modular trailer carrying a 100 tonne transformer which was one of three identical loads shipped into Southampton's Trafalgar dock from Italy during June 1984 for the J.E.T. project at Culham, near Didcot. Pickfords Heavy Haulage changed its title to Pickfords Industrial during December 1981 to reflect the company's active involvement in factory machinery re-location and electrical engineering. *D. Kinsella*

Left: Rated for 200 tonne operation was this Scammell S26 6x4 tractor fitted with a Cummins 350hp engine and Brockhouse torque converter. It entered service with Sunters of Northallerton during 1984 and is seen here coupled to a Nicolas 2 bed 4 modular trailer about to leave the works of Motherwell Bridge with a 60 tonne pressure vessel for delivery to Inverness. This unit passed on into Econofreight ownership during the amalgamation of that company with Sunters and Wynns during May 1986.

Above: Leylands T45 Roadtrain cab by Motor Panels featured on most Scammell products from 1980. Although badged as a Leyland this Hawkins Plant Hire S26-35 was underneath a Scammell product being built at Watford. Rated for 100 tonne operation the 6x4 tractor featured a Cummins NTE 350 engine and Eaton Fuller gearbox. Based in Wem, Shropshire, the vehicle is photographed delivering a 42 tonne Caterpillar 631D motor scraper into Plymouth airport during May 1987 to assist in the construction of a new runway. Its tri axle low loader was the product of Watson trailers.

Right: The South West Division of the Central Electricity Generating Board used a pair of these Scammell S24 6x4 tractors to transport irradiated nuclear waste in the form of used uranium fuel rods from its Hinkley Point power station to a nearby railhead transfer facility at Bridgwater. Entering service during 1982 the 100 ton capacity tractors pulled specifically built flask low loaders manufactured by Crane Fruehauf which were designed for 60 tonne operation. The Cummins NTE 350 engined tractors featured Allison automatic transmissions with torque converters. Further modifications adapted to compensate for low speed operation were the fitment of twin radiators each with its own fan and Kysor shutters.

Above: Photographed making steady progress along the A27 in West Sussex during October 1979 were Keighley based heavy haulier James Watkinson. Using a Cometto 3 bed 6 modular trailer to accommodate a 120 ton pre-stressed concrete support beam, the outfit was heading for Goodwood Racecourse near Winchester where a new tiered grandstand was under construction. Traction came primarily from a Mercedes Titan 2632 6x6 unit - new into the U.K. and still bearing a German registration number while on evaluation by Watkinsons. However when circumstances dictated a Scania LBT 140 6x4 ballasted tractor was used to 'double head' along the route as shown here.

Right: This fine example of a V8 powered Scania LBT 141 6x4 tractor was once operated by Lawsons Haulage of Cockermouth, Cumbria. Distinctive with its Dutch 'flat-top' cab the unit was originally owned by Zwagerman BV in Holland who used it to move fully rigged cranes with their jibs protruding over the front cab - hence the lower height. The tractor was imported to the U.K. by Harry Baines (of Rotinoff fame) based near Blackpool and subsequently sold on to Lawsons. Its load here is a 65 tonne Caterpillar 245ME excavator riding upon a 4 axle Transquip low loader. *D. Tomlin*

Above: Transports Cauvas from France have long been enthusiastic operators of Scania tractors including this early Vabis LB76 4x2 sleeper cabbed unit seen inbound at Southampton's ferry terminal in June 1978. Its unique elderly rear steer low loader which was probably a Kaiser strongly suggestive German designs (possibly Scheuerle) with exposed steering link arms. The load which was 11ft in diameter and weighed 6 tons, when assembled would be described as a steel sealing ring.

Right: Coleman & Company of Stechford, Birmingham, are demolition specialists and once owned this Scania 142E double drive tractor powered by a V8 14 litre engine. Seen here at Southampton docks during September 1986, the vehicle had hauled this NCK Ajax crawler crane from the Midlands aboard a tri axle Task low loader. This unit was replaced during 1993 by a MAN 6x4 tractor. *D. Kinsella*

Norman Keedwell of Burnham-on-Sea in Somerset is the proud owner of this well presented 1985 Scania 142E 6x4 tractor unit. Fitted with a 450bhp V8 engine driving through a 15 speed Fuller deep reduction gearbox, the vehicle sports detailed paintwork depicting the work it undertakes. It is seen in June 1999 negotiating Paignton seafront where a 32 tonne CMI 3-70C Trashmaster landfill compactor had been loaded out of a Waste Management exhibition. The Bridgwater bound machine was aboard Keedwell's heavily modified 4 axle Watson low loader incorporating a Dyson swan-neck.

Although hardly required to move this small transformer out of Plymouth's redundant power station, Graham Keedwell's (brother of Norman) Scania 142E 10x4 tractor can handle loads up to 150 tonnes capacity. TUG 324W began life as a 6x4 prior to conversion to a 8x4 specification back in 1990. Now re-badged as a 146E it was again modified into a 5 axle unit during April 1995 by Miles Nunn of Whitchurch which involved the fitment of an additional lifting Hendrickson rear axle. Power comes via a Scania V8 420 bhp engine driven through a 15 speed Fuller gearbox.

Above: Withdrawn from service in June 1998 Colletts Scania LT146 8x4 tractor certainly turned some heads in its lifetime. The ex Watkinson 450hp unit was employed in the movement of four bridge and boom girders transported to Canada Dock, Liverpool during 1994. Loaded in Bolton the 177ft long steel beams weighed 70 tonnes apiece and were heading for Charleston, Carolina, U.S.A. to form new ship to shore quayside container handling cranes then under construction. Running with a ballast box BDB 369T is shown during June of that year moving one of these loads which was being supported at either end by a set of 6 row Nicolas and Cometto bogies fitted with turntables. *D. Tomlin*

Left: Entering service with Watkinson Lifting and Transportation during May 1996 was this 150 tonne capacity 420hp Scania T142E 6x4 tractor. Replaced by a new MAN unit during 2000 the Scania is shown here moving a 42 tonne Vickers AS90 self propelled 155mm gun from Topcliffe, North Yorkshire to Salisbury during August 1997. The location was Jacks Hill Café on the A5 near Towcester and the trailer being used was a 60 tonne capacity 4 axle rear steer Goldhofer. *R. Tew*

127

Above: Geoff Kilbey Heavy Haulage of New Milton, Hampshire acquired the ex Hills of Botley 150 tonne Scania 143E 8x4 tractor during June 1999. One of its first jobs for its new owner was the movement of this Ruston Bucyrus 600SC crawler crane from Devonport to Southampton. Grossing nearly 90 tonnes the haul was undertaken with the assistance of a 4 axle Nooteboom rear steer low loader.

Left: This Scania 143E 8x4 tractor was one of a pair to enter service with McIntosh Heavy Haulage of Dunecht, Aberdeen during 1995. N500 MPH is pictured at work during November 1999 at Barton Services on the A1 whilst moving this NCK Eiger crawler crane body from Peterhead to Middlesbrough. The 450hp tractor is normally matched with this Nooteboom 4 axle rear steer low loader. *S. Pearson*

Above: Curtis Heavy Haulage are pictured on the A1 (M) Washington Services during April 1999 with their Scania 143E 6x4 150 tonne capacity tractor 'Lady Charlotte'. Its load was the lower pedestal slew ring from Saren's 2000 tonne Demag PC 9600 crane weighing 60 tonnes. Pulling 6 lines of Goldhofer modular axles, the tractor was ballasted with some of the crane's counterweights to move it from Middlesbrough to the BP refinery at Grangemouth. This particular unit bought new during 1989, was one of a batch of 143E tractors originally built for Italy but was subsequently cancelled, thus explaining the left hand drive arrangement.

Right: During April 1999 Collett Heavy Transport moved this 62 tonne pressure vessel from Halifax to Grangemouth using a Scheuerle Inter-Combi 2 bed 3 modular trailer. As a result of a Scheuerle/Nooteboom marketing alliance formed in 1998 the two trailer companies now have the facilities to jointly offer a wider range of modular equipment to operators with a capacity of up to 1000 tonnes. The Scania 143E 400hp 6x4 unit is good for 150 tonne operation and sports a unique double sleeper cab conversion undertaken in June 1995 by a Manchester based company.

132   Photographed conquering the notoriously steep Haldon Hill on the A38 just south of Exeter is this Scania 143E 6x4 unit belonging to Gallacher Brothers of Stanley, County Durham. Formerly owned by Derek Parnaby the vehicle retained its original livery depicting murals of vehicles formerly operated by the company. Parnaby's were also responsible for the creation of the truck's heavily modified front grille and bumper arrangement. The load being moved here during April 1994 upon a tri axle Andover trailer was a 40 tonne ships winch, en route from Newcastle to Devonport dockyard.

P414 TGG was one of four new Scania 3 series tractor units which entered the Blantyre based Cadzow Heavy Haulage fleet in Scotland during 1997. The 143E 450hp tractor was the only 8x4 in the batch having undergone a fourth axle conversion by North East Truck & Van, making it capable of 150 tonne operation. May 2000 saw the unit moving this Terex TS24B twin engined motor scraper from Earls Colne, Essex to Derby with the assistance of a 4 axle Goldhofer rear steer low loading trailer. *S. Pearson*

Originally operated in Germany by Brewer, this Scania 143E 8x4 tractor is unusual in that it sports a '3 series' Streamline cab - an option which was not readily available on the company's heavy duty 'E' type tractors. Owned by GCS Johnson of Richmond since July 1998, the left hand drive unit was utilised to move this 100 tonne rotor from Newcastle to London during September 1998 aboard a Nicolas 2 bed 4 modular trailer. Plated for 210 tonne operation, the unit is fitted with a second steer/lifting axle and 500hp engine driving through a torque converter and retarder. *R. Tew*

This 150 tonne capacity Scania 144G 8x4 Topline cabbed tractor entered service with Transport Co Partnership of Bradford in June 2000. The unit began life as a 6x4 being converted into an eight wheeler by an Austrian Scania dealer from where the vehicle was purchased - hence the Austrian registration. Uprated to 580hp, the tractor is regularly employed on abnormal load movements throughout Europe and Eastern Bloc countries. The vehicle is seen on this occasion at Dartford Europort ferry terminal in July 2000 outward bound for Salzgitter, Germany with a 59 tonne furnace that had been collected from the manufacturer's premises in Oxted, Surrey. The 18ft wide load was moved aboard a 4 axle Faymonville rear steer 60 tonne capacity low loader. *L. Rogers*

Above: Scania introduced its '4 series' range onto the U.K. market during 1996, its heavy haulage tractors being designated 'G' class models with engine variants ranging from a modest 220bhp to the mighty 530hp V8. J.B.Rawcliffe & Sons of Mawdesley, Lancashire, put this 144G 460bhp tractor on the road during November 1998. It was converted into 8x4 specification in the company's own workshops and fitted with a heavy duty front bumper incorporating a set of towing/pushing jaws. July 1999 saw S298 LFV manoeuvring into Forge Tech's premises in Ashton-under-Lyme having transported this 125 tonne casting from Sheffield for machining. Grossing nearly 200 tonnes, the move utilised 11 rows of Nicolas modular axles. *D. Tomlin*

Left: This impressive four series Scania is a 530hp 144G double drive tractor in service with Rotherham based Hol-Tro Heavy Haulage. Sporting a high roof Topline cab, the unit normally runs with this 4 axle Nooteboom rear steer low loader moving Brown Lenox Pegson crushing plant around the U.K. and Europe. This 26 tonne BL-Pegson Eurotrak 900x600 tracked mobile crusher had just been loaded out of Hillhead Quarry's heavy plant show at Buxton during June 1999. *R. Tew*

137

Above: The first two factory built Scania R144G 8x4 heavy haulage tractors to enter service with a U. K. haulier joined the fleet of McIntosh Heavy Logistics of Westhill, Aberdeenshire during October 1999. Rated for 150 tonne operation T400 MPH and T500 MPH are fitted with Scania's 14 litre 460hp V8 engine which drives through a 12 speed gearbox featuring a hydraulic retarder. The load picture here is a cable reel relating to the offshore oil exploration industry riding on a 4 axle rear steer Nooteboom trailer, one of ten various types owned by McIntosh.

Right: Scotts Heavy Haulage (Ireland) are actually based in Alfreton, Derbyshire and operate a pair of Scania 144G Topline cabbed tractors including this 530hp factory built 8x4 unit rated for 150 tonne GCW. This picture was taken in the company's yard during August 2000 and shows the tractor pulling a 4 axle Nooteboom rear steer extendable low loader. Sat aboard it was a 37 tonne Ideaco 8x8 mobile gas drilling rig en route from Lincoln to Golden Pot, near Alton, Hampshire. *A. Goodman*

Above: This impressive Scania 144G 8x4 Topline cabbed tractor is owned by Dutch marine transport specialists Van De Wetering B.V. of Loosdrecht. Pictured having just loaded a Princess 460 luxury motorboat at its builders, Marine Projects, in Plymouth during May 1998, at 460hp the vehicle was well up to the task of delivering the vessel to its new owners in Caen, France. The 12ft wide load was carried upon a tri axle Broshuis extendable trailer specially built for boat transportation. The load shipped to France via the Portsmouth ro/ro facility.

Right: P6 LTS, a Scania 144G 460bhp tractor was new to Heanor Haulage during January 1997. It gained an additional fourth non driven axle eighteen months later, giving it a rating of 150 tonnes gross combination weight. March 1999, however, saw the unit hauling this 225 tonne dressed CO_2 stripper vessel a short distance from Fabricom Engineering at Immingham to the Nordic Terminal for onward export to Norway. Ballasted to 40 tonnes, the tractor was pulling a Cometto telescopic beam modular trailer fitted with sets of 6 and 5 rows of modular axles. *A. Goodman.*

Heanor Haulage put a pair of these 150 tonne capacity Scania 144G 8x4 530hp tractors into service during late 1998. Registered S623 JAL and S624 JAL the units underwent typical 'Heanor conversions' into 4 axle tractors with the fitment of Italian built air suspended lifting second axles. Telma electromagnetic retarders were also specified. Coupled to a 110 tonne capacity Nooteboom 5 axle rear steer beam deck trailer featuring a tandem axle jeep dolly, S623 JAL was used to move a 73 tonne Caterpillar 990 wheeled loading shovel from Leicester to Ketton during June 1999. *A. Goodman*

When H. Frost & Sons of Bury St. Edmunds purchased their Scania T124L 400hp 4x2 tractor, they converted it in their own workshops into 6x2 specification with the fitment of an additional mid lift axle. The unit is pictured here on Rothersthorpe Services (M1) during August 1999 moving a 24 tonne GKN Warrior AIFV (Armoured Infantry Fighting Vehicle) from Louth to Salisbury Plain, Wiltshire. Rated for 65 tonne operation, the Scania was coupled to a Nooteboom tri axle step frame trailer. *R. Tew*

Above: Scania's T cabbed bonneted four series tractors quickly gained recognition with British hauliers and some are now appearing in U.K. heavy haulage fleets. One of the finest examples has to be this unit owned by A & I Freight of Burscough, Lancashire. New to the company in April 1999 the 150 tonne 144G 530hp 6x4 tractor is matched to a 100 tonne capacity King 4 axle low loader fitted with a tandem axle jeep dolly. Photographed in June that year in Bachy's yard at Ormskirk it is loaded with a 65 tonne Casagrande C90 tracked piling rig for delivery to Maidstone, Kent. *D. Tomlin*

Left: Photographed during August 2000 moving an electro motor gearbox housing from the former Blue Circle cement works in Plymouth was H.C. Wilson's Elmswell based Scania T144G 6x4 tractor. Rated for 90 tonne operation and coupled to a tri axle Nooteboom step frame trailer, the unit originated from the Belgian company Berger. It was purchased by Wilson's during September 1999 from a dealer in Cheltenham. With the personal registration mark R100 HCW, the 530 hp unit runs on air suspension and is regularly employed on continental abnormal load work.

145

Above: Stiller Transport of Darlington purchased a trio of these 32 ton GCW Seddon Atkinson 400 series 4x2 tractors during 1981 and put them into service on long load work. With the temporary fitment of a Rymar non driven additional tag axle attached to the tractor's fifth wheel it uprated the Cummins NTC 290bhp powered units to 6x2 spec. enabling heavier loads to be transported. Rymar were also responsible for building the extendable pole trailer featured here with a tri axle rear steer bogie moving three 60ft long concrete roof trusses from Teeside to Gloucester during 1983.

Left: February 1999 saw this 460hp Scania T144L 6x2 tractor join the Ascroft Transport fleet based in Tarleton, Preston. Originally a cancelled order, the 66 tonne capacity tractor is used primarily to move Caterpillar equipment throughout the country on behalf of U.K. distributors Finning. Shown here hitched to a Nooteboom tri axle step frame trailer its load consisted of a Cat 924G wheeled loading shovel and a 216 skid steer loader moved from Torbay to Cardiff during June 2000.

Above: Things have come a long way since this Seddon 34 Four 4x2 day cabbed tractor was classed as a top of the range long distance truck. Powered by a modest 204hp Cummins NH220, the model was introduced in 1969 being one of the lightest units available to U.K. operators at that time. Operated by Southampton Road Transport on the Pirelli cable contract this unit was seen during September 1974 at the docks pulling a tandem axle 25 ton capacity Tasker low loader carrying a large 14ft diameter wooden drum containing 15 tons of underwater cable.

Right: Steyr-Daimler-Puch have been building trucks since 1922 and are Austria's leading heavy vehicle manufacturer. Its distinctive wedge shaped tilt cab was introduced in 1968 and continued in production well into the Eighties. The 19 S 31 tractor featured here has a 6x2 conversion and is one of several Steyrs owned by Somerset haulier Martin Hayman of Burlescombe who specialises in the transport of agricultural machinery. The vehicle was moving a pair of Renault tractors when photographed near Haymans base during March 1999. The models loaded aboard the tri axle step frame York trailer were a 610RZ and a 340X.

148

Above: French heavy haulier Transports P. Cussonneau used this V8 powered Unic Izoard 6x4 tractor on cross channel abnormal load work when seen in February 1979. Under a marketing agreement with Fiat in the late sixties, many Unic designs used Fiat components including cabs, so whilst obviously not young, this example seems to be wearing very well. The load is a 43 ton press sat aboard a tri axle Nicolas low loader featuring a rear steer independent dolly and substantial heavy duty deck beams with fixed swan-necks.

Left: Over 1,000 Thornycrofts were produced at the company's works in Basingstoke, the British Army taking around four hundred of those. Gradually replaced in favour of the Scammell Commander during the mid eighties, the Mk3 'Mighty Antar' featured here boasted a Rolls Royce 16 litre C8 diesel engine with a Supercharger pumping out 333hp - not much by today's standards. Its tandem axle '8 in line' Sankey trailer was capable of moving 60 tons, so its 55 ton Centurion main battle tank fell just within its limits. All up weight of a fully laden outfit tipped the scales at approximately 90 tons. This particular load was being moved from M.V.E.E. Chertsey to 18 A.M.T.U. at Bovington Camp in Dorset when photographed at Weyhill, near Andover during August 1979.

Above: One of the most impressive vehicles to emerge from Unipower was N523 YAJ. Primarily acting as a demonstrator with Econofreight during 1995 the Cummins 14 litre powered 6x6 tractor proved so successful that it was purchased by the company. The truck was given its revised Econofreight livery in the Middlesborough workshops during 1996 where it also underwent a high roof crew cab conversion. Rated for 240 tonne operation its 465hp engine drives through a 16 speed ZF gearbox and WSK 400 torque converter. December 1998 saw the unit hauling a 180 tonne gas turbine generator out of Immingham docks destined for the Stallingborough power station using 16 rows of Nicolas platform trailer. *R. Tew*

Right: It did not take long for Volvo to firmly establish themselves as a respected manufacturer of rugged heavy duty tractors through the Seventies. Arguably the models that won the orders were the company's F88/89 range of which a pair of the latter found their way into the Billingham based Magnaload fleet during 1976. Rated for 180 ton operation NPY 439P and RAJ 530R are pictured during December 1979 coupled to a 12 row Scheuerle modular trailer carrying a 130 ton Cowans Sheldon railway crane from Carlisle to Workington for onward export to New Zealand.

154

The first U.K. registered Volvo F86 cabbed tractor unit entered service in 1967 with a Tyneside operator, a deal which paved the way for Volvo's establishment in Britain. The F86 only ever underwent minor modification during its production life, the most significant of these being the revised grille and redesigned interior introduced during 1973. One of those later models is seen here a year later when the Portswood main drainage scheme was under construction in Southampton. This Archimedean screw had just arrived on site during December having been imported from its Dutch builders via Felixstowe docks. Transported by Coastal Roadways the load weighed 14 tons, measured 55ft long and could bore a 9ft diameter hole.

E. F. Phillips of Parkstone near Poole ran a very diverse fleet of vehicles ranging from tippers to skip-loaders and a European operation based in Southampton. This outfit was the largest vehicle in the fleet, a Volvo FB88 6x4 unit which spent much of its time engaged on heavy plant movement. However on this occasion during November 1974 its load consisted of a section of recycling plant being transported from Poole to Rouen, France aboard a Crane Fruehauf tandem axle low loader. Phillips were bought out by the Drinkwater Group during the late eighties and they continued to operate the waste removal side of the business from the Parkstone depot.

Above: The Volvo F88 quickly gained popularity in Britain's general and heavy haulage fleets alike. This example was a 290hp 6x4 100 tonner, which was to enjoy a very varied life. Bought secondhand by M. J. Rolls of Cambridge it eventually passed on into the Robinsons Heavy Haulage fleet of Sandy, Beds. After undergoing a major refurbishment by this company the vehicle eventually moved on to another owner in Cornwall, C. J. Vincent & Son of Fraddon who now use the tractor to transport the company's traction engine to rallies. RLL 618R is shown here in M J. Rolls ownership delivering a 23 ton Caterpillar 16 motor grader to Southampton docks for export using a tri axle Task low loader. *D. Kinsella*

Right: Peterborough Heavy Haulage of Yaxley were the operators of this 100 ton Volvo F88 6x4 290hp tractor photographed during April 1977. Sat upon its tandem axle King rear steer low loader is a 26 ton Aveling Barford Centaur dumptruck arriving at Southampton docks for export. Such loads were often dropped off at this point and then driven up the linkspan under their own power onto the ship. On occasions, however, particularly if the machine was tracked or immobile the complete low loader was reversed up onto the ship's exposed deck where abnormal loads were accommodated, and unloaded there.

Above: New to Chelmsford Plant Hire in 1982 this Volvo F12 150 ton capacity tractor ended up in the Heavyhaul (Chelmsford) fleet. Powered by a 330hp engine PME 728X is seen during 1992 moving an aircraft fuselage from Southend to Moreton-in-the-Marsh fire service training centre in Gloucestershire. The plane wings were moved separately and re-assembled at the load's destination, where the aircraft was to be used to train fire-fighting personnel. The trailer used for the 'Hot Air' move was a tri axle King semi low extendable. Now replaced by a FH12 6x4 unit, the F12 is no longer in operation, but will always be remembered for giving 16 years of trouble free service. *P. Dyke*

Right: A rather unusual load being transported along the M5 Motorway in Somerset when seen during June 1998 was this 65 tonne Wirtgen SP 1600 slipform paving machine. Its haulier was Keighley based MSM Heavy Transport who used a 150 tonne capacity Volvo F12 6x4 tractor to move the machine from Leeds to Honiton, Devon. Grossing around 110 tonnes, the 2 bed 4 modular low loader was the product of Nicolas.

Above: Danny Teasdale of Bawtry, Nottinghamshire operated this unusual Volvo N12 385hp 6x2 sleeper cabbed tractor on abnormal load work from 1997 to 1999. Rated for 80 tonne operation the truck is pictured waiting to unload a 50 tonne 90ft long concrete bridge beam in Blythe, one of several which had been hauled up from Peterborough to form the deck of a new flyover construction. This tractor featured a Robson drive system which temporarily converts the 6x2 unit into double drive. The set up utilises an idler cog friction wheel which is lowered between the drive and lift axle bogie tyres, thus revolving both axles together, transmitting useful extra traction - a practice commonly used in Scandinavia. When the Volvo was eventually sold to a dealer, it was to re-appear touring the U.K. with the American Circus.

Right: In July 1998 Abnormal Load Engineering of Stafford moved three of these condensers from Richborough power station to nearby Ramsgate docks for onward export to Indonesia. The load shown had dimensions of 20ft wide, 23ft high and weighed approx 200 tonnes. Sat aboard a 12 row Nicolas modular platform trailer this particular load was originally hauled by another tractor but due to a breakdown the Volvo N1227 was pushed into service as a towing tractor. Originally attending as 'double heading/back-up unit', KEH 838N performed well. It was bought secondhand by ALE from Norway and its normal role within the company involved delivering empty modular trailers to site and rigging duties, being ideally equipped with its rear mounted crane and heavy duty winch. *R. Tew*

162

This Volvo F12 8x4 tractor originally began life as a standard 6x4 F89 cabbed unit with Exeter heavy haulier Wally Balsdon registered KPP 279P. The fourth axle conversion and cab transplant was undertaken in Balsdons Poltimore workshops during 1989 and the vehicle remained in service with them for seven years. It then passed on into the Bob Francis Crane Hire fleet based in Rhuddlan, North Wales where it was re-registered with the Irish number RIW 2839. During July 1997 the truck moved this 70 tonne O& K RH30D excavator using a 4 axle Nooteboom low loader fitted with a Broshuis neck. The unit has since been sold and converted for heavy recovery work.

Plymouth based PAP International specialise in trans-European marine transport, but in July 1999, the company was performing locally, moving this boat hull through the streets of the city from Lee Mill to Stonehouse. The 20ft wide load was carried upon a Belgian built EKW tri axle extendable trailer pulled by a Volvo F12 6x2 Globetrotter tractor. The boat was moved via a specific high load route that required the temporary removal of several pieces of street furniture and traffic signals to ease its passage.

Above: This Volvo F16 8x4 Globetrotter cabbed tractor was originally new to Cliffe Plant of Rochester. Plated for 200 tonne operation it eventually passed on into the fleet of H.E. Services based in nearby Strood. After a short period of operation there it was acquired by Heanor Haulage of Langley Mill during February 1997 and consequently received its third coat of paint into their colours. The load it is moving here is a 110 tonne 'undressed' CO_2 stripper column out of the Nordic terminal on Humberside into the works of Immingham based Fabricom Engineering during April 1999. The 500hp tractor utilised a Cometto 13 row modular trailer for the short haul featuring a telescopic connecting beam. *A. Goodman*

Left: Photographed at Brent Knoll Services on the M5 was Exeter based heavy haulier Wally Balsdon who were once part of the South West Crane Hire group. Grossing 125 tonnes, the load consisted of an 85 tonne Caterpillar 992C wheeled loading shovel being moved from St. Austell, Cornwall, to Tilbury Docks for onward export to Greece. The 150 tonne capacity Volvo F16 6x4 Globetrotter is ex-Wrekin Transport and was pulling a King TL90/15 90 tonne capacity 4 axle beam deck low loader featuring a 'load divider' dolly.

Above: Replacing an ageing DAF 95 series in June 1997 was this well presented Volvo FH12 6x4 Globetrotter tractor owned by Redditch based Mining and Piling Limited. One of its first jobs involved moving this NCK Pennine crawler crane down to Plymouth where it was to be used on piling duties for a major tunnelling project. The vehicle is shown pulling a tri axle King low loader accommodating the load, awaiting a police escort into the city from Smithaleigh on the A38.

Left: John Coles of Langtree, North Devon put this 150 tonne capacity Volvo FH16 6x4 Globetrotter double drive tractor into service during October 1998. The truck is pictured at Lewdown on the A30 near Launceston, Cornwall, transporting a 48 tonne Caterpillar 345B excavator with the aid of an Andover tri axle low loader. The machine, collected at Hingston Down Quarry at Gunnislake, was en route to a new job in Gloucester. The FH joined another F16 in the Coles Plant Hire fleet, both being primarily employed moving the company's earth moving equipment to and from site.

Above: The first Volvo FH Series tractor to be converted into 8x4 specification went into service with Banks Brothers of West Carnforth, County Durham, during October 1997. Powered by a 420hp engine, the FH12 Globetrotter is rated for 150 tonnes GTW and was built originally in Sweden as a 6x4 unit. Its fourth axle conversion was undertaken by North East Truck and Van of Teeside and features air suspension enabling it to lift and self track. Another first for Banks was the acquisition of its Faymonville Megamax trailer, it being the first of its type to enter U.K. service. With a payload of 100 tonnes, the 5 axle rear steering low loader easily accommodates the 60 tonne Caterpillar 777B dumptruck illustrated.

Left: This Dutch barge measuring 73ft in length was transported from Warwick to Dijon, France, during October 1998 by Offshore Transport Services of Scunthorpe. The 77 tonne haul was undertaken by a Volvo FH12 6x2 tractor coupled to a Broshuis 6 axle semi-low extendable trailer with rear steering. The load was shipped out of the U.K. via the ro/ro ferry facility connecting Portsmouth with Caen where the vehicle is pictured. *F. Naylor*

Above: Running in the Volvo dominated fleet of Bristol based Kings Heavy Haulage is P109 THW, a Volvo FH16 6x4 Globetrotter unit, one of three such types currently operated. Although rated for 150 tonne operation the 520hp tractor used very little effort to move this 15ft wide Royal Marines landing craft out of Turnchapel, Plymouth, during March 1998. The 20 tonne load was moved to Instow, North Devon, aboard a 4 axle rear steer low loader built by Faymonville of Belgium.

Right: Pulling a King 4 axle beam deck low loader fitted with a single axle 'load divider' dolly is this ex L.C. Lewis Volvo FH16 6x4 tractor capable of 150 tonnes GTW operation. The load in this May 1999 movement was a 65 tonne Caterpillar 245B excavator. Wally Balsdon of Exeter were the transporters of the machine, which was heading for Bedminster, Bristol. Balsdon became part of the South West Crane Hire group during late 1997 but its low loaders were subsequently 'sold off' during 2000.

Above: New to Keelby, Lincolnshire based heavy haulier John Somerscales in May 1999 was this impressive 150 tonne capacity Volvo FH16 6x4 unit. Fitted with a high roof Globetrotter XL cab and extended wheelbase, the 520hp tractor is moving a 45 tonne Omtrac mobile stone crusher out of the Hillhead Quarry plant show at Buxton the following July. Loaded aboard a tri axle Nooteboom trailer, the machine was destined for Italy. *R. Tew*

Right: This outfit belonging to demolition specialists Brown and Mason of Birchington, Kent was photographed at the former Blue Circle cement works in Plymstock, Plymouth, the company winning the contract to demolish the complex. The first big machine to be delivered was this 75 tonne Komatsu PC 750 SE excavator which was to be fitted with a long reach boom. The machine had been hauled from Liverpool by this Volvo FH16 6x4 Globetrotter 150 tonne capacity tractor which in turn was coupled to a Nooteboom 4 axle rear steer low loader fitted with a tandem axle jeep dolly.

Above: In the period April through to July 2000, Langley Mill based Heanor Haulage took delivery of four new 145 tonne capacity 6x4 Volvo FH16 Globetrotter tractors fitted with air suspension. One of the 6x4 FH16's - W551 HJW - is shown at Sandbach Services on the M6 moving an NCK Eiger crawler crane body from Liverpool to Derby during May 2000. The 5 axle beam deck rear steer Nooteboom trailer was fitted with a tandem axle dolly and rated for 110 tonne capacity. Both units that actually entered service as 6x4 tractors are destined for conversion into 8x4 tractors at a future date.

Left: This 6x4 Globetrotter cabbed Volvo FH!6 heavy haulage tractor rated for 150 tonne operation entered service during September 1995 with Allsop (Plant & Haulage) of Smalley, Derbyshire. Sitting on its Nooteboom 4 axle trailer and jeep dolly when photographed at rest on Woodall Services (M1) during August 1999 was the top half of a Demag H185S mining excavator. At nearly 18ft wide and grossing 116 tonnes, the load had been collected in Durham and was en route to a Bardon quarry in Leicestershire. When fully assembled the 1346hp Demag weighs in at around 225 tonnes. *R. Tew*

175

Two of Heanors batch of 145 tonne Volvo FH16 6x4 units purchased during a four month period in 2000 were immediately converted in the company's own workshops to 8x4 specification, these being registered W553 HJW and W554 HJW. one example of the two converted is shown here having just loaded a 67 tonne Junttan PM25 tracked piling rig at Par Docks, Cornwall during June 2000. This load was about to be moved to Doncaster aboard a 4 axle Trailmaster trailer fitted with King neck.